Vantage Point:
A Personal
Essay Book

D1738553

Megan Hubrex

First edition April 2023
ISBN: 9798375230825
Imprint: Independently Published

This book is dedicated to my Grandma Judi, who always pushed me to be creative as possible.

You are a sunflower in a field of wilting daisies.

-C.E.M

Table of Contents

Do People Ever Read the Foreword Before the Book Starts?

I wrote my first book, Welcome to the Middle, Kid, in 2018. It was messy and poorly written and if you still own it, throw it away because it was awful. I decided to change it around and wrote The One Who Stayed: An Autobiographical Essay Book. I can no longer read that book either because of how much I cringe at my writing. I love the story I told, and my past never changed, but I have grown as a writer. I wrote my second book, The Art of Talking, in 2020. That book wasn't about me; it was an interview book about other people (I'm still debating whether I like it or not...) But each time I write a book, I absolutely love it. The adrenaline, the platform to get my writing out there, and the kindness I receive after it all. It is addicting in the best way.

I knew I wanted to try my first book over, although I have done that many times. The aspect of an essay book has always intrigued me since I'm a "short but sweet" writer. I have a hard time writing fiction and I can't write real long chapters. The One

Who Stayed didn't include true essays, though, and I wanted to finally achieve that type of book.

You are currently about to read my first *real* essay book.

Some of these essays include stories from my first book, but they are rewritten in a way that they deserve.

I have grown as a writer, as I've said, and I've grown as a person, which is most important of all. This book includes my life in short story form, but like many people in this world, my life wasn't always sunshine and surface level.

There *are* trigger warnings throughout this book: medical misconduct, grief, self-doubt, and some language not suitable for my mother.

But there is also happiness, joy, and love.

I am a person willing to share all of me and I hope you'll take me as I am.

Lots of love,

Megan Hubrex

Here's Why

All I hear in the small, gray room is my pencil scratching on paper. A dull, yellow, number 2 pencil with no eraser. Did someone chew it off? Or maybe they erased their feelings so much that it dwindled down to nothing.

The paper I was using was the back of a worksheet that stated "you'll get better. Here's how." I've never written about my heart before. About how my soul was aching at that very moment. As I laid on my hard mattress, I used Carrie Fisher's book I just read, aptly named Shockaholic, as a hard surface to write on. There wasn't a chair in my room, although there was a desk. Probably because chairs were a threat to staff. We could throw them at any moment, at any person. We needed to be safe at all costs. Our minds needed to be protected.

I start scribbling words on the paper. It turned into some sort of poetry, I think. I was not good at writing poems; I didn't even enjoy writing in general. I used to get decent grades in school English classes, but it amounted to nothing. Except at that certain moment, in that hospital, I wrote. I switched from poetry to making lists of what I would do when I got out of there. I ended up needing another worksheet. I crept out of my room, stepped carefully in my gripped socks and sweatpants with no strings, and snuck into the community room where no one ever used it outside of group therapy. I found a crumpled worksheet that stated "your feelings are valid. Here's why" and stepped back into my room.

I started writing again.

"I understand why I'm here. I don't want to be held like a prisoner. I'm the most positive person here. I hate myself." I scratched and scrawled, and it turned into a journal entry. I tried keeping a diary when I was young, but it never lasted long. I remember writing about how much I loved the Jonas Brothers and how I didn't get any role at summer theater camp because I was a bad singer. This, though, was different. I wrote small and I wrote fast. I poured my heart and head into this entry. I decided right then that I was going to start a mental health blog when I broke out of that place. A place to harbor this outlet.

In this big, window filled building and in this small, white walled room, I discovered writing.

By day, I would fill out the front of worksheets that stated "you can get help. Here's where" and by night, I was connecting the dots of who I was and who I wanted to become. A writer never passed my mind, even when everyone wanted me to go to college for an English degree. When I had nothing, no private bathroom, constant 15-minute check ins, and no sound mind, I suddenly had writing.

Big Words Don't Make You Taller:

An essay response for my 2022 English class

What the hell was this? We just read _____ by _____ for class. I haven't read many essays, per say, but this was arguably the worst I've ever read. This author wrote a bunch of shit about eyesight that was repetitive and worthy of a textbook, yet she is banking off this garbage because it's "profound." That's an opinion I don't have. Yet, I can't speak that if I don't want the professor or certain students to fight be about "how beautiful" her metaphors are. I thought the person in the essay was blind, for God's Sakes! Turns out, she's very much not?! Why do people write stories and essays that need to be interpreted to enjoy? I need something between The Very Hungry Caterpillar and this author.

Bigger metaphors don't make you cool.

A Child Cries

In a small suburb of Illinois, USA, in the year 1998, a 5-year-old child cries. Was this poor girl crying because she was hurt? Physically, no. Emotionally, yes. The 5-year-old saw her mother give other children attention at her own birthday party. This was not something the child would willing put up with, this nicety. So, she did what any other 5-year-old would not do: she told her mother that she wanted to die.

Now, it is widely debated whether this hurt girl said that statement after the party or during the party. It doesn't really matter, as it was still said, nonetheless. She used to watch Barney and shows for children; there was no way she could've picked it up from somewhere else. Who would even speak that way in front of a child long enough for the said child to repeat it?

As the months passed after the birthday party, the cute 5-year-old started drawing pictures of her and her family, except she would cross herself out with a big X. On walks with her mom, and while they held hands, the child would tell her mother she wanted to die. Was this innocent girl saying this because her baby brother was just born, and she couldn't handle sharing the love? Was it because they recently moved from Texas to a suburb of Chicago? Or was she simply being a child drama queen? No one knew what brought it on.

The blonde, chubby cheeked little girl, of course, was the last to know something was even wrong. She started going to strange doctors to appease her parents and she was repeatedly asked by people she didn't know if she ever saw smiley faces on the walls.

This small child either had an attention seeking complex or something was rooted more deeply within her tiny body. No one at that time knew what was to come in her future.

The happy-go-lucky little girl in this story had no idea the severity of the storm on the sea that was about to be conjured and she didn't know how to build a boat.

God Moment

When I hiked across the Cliffs of Moher in Ireland, on a stone path with room for only one person at a time to walk, I didn't think the trip would be worth all the heavy breathing I was doing. My mother had to turn around as her knees could not take the terrain, so my dad and I trudged on. We ended up on a semi flat open cliff with no railing and I kept staring straight ahead as thoughts danced around whether I wanted to keep hiking. We were ¾ the way to the very top, but everyone was seemingly stopping on this cliff. When I finally turned around to see why this cliff was so popular, I looked at what we just climbed.

I saw what nature made. The vast green and gray colored cliffs with the roaring sea hitting the rock below. A rainbow appeared above the sea spray, and it moved me to my core. My mom once told me that seeing the Grand Canyon for the first time was her "God Moment" as she was so astounded by what He made.

The Cliffs of Moher was my God moment.

I was in awe of the sheer beauty, and I was in awe of life itself. The realization that I am a tiny speck on this beautiful Earth was humbling.

I stood there, quietly absorbing what I was seeing, and I moved just enough to capture a picture.

Me and My Brain

I had brain surgery in 2015. They put me to sleep with medication that celebrities die from, they poked at my brain, then they pushed me to my car in a wheelchair as I audibly wept in unbearable pain.

I had 16 of those surgeries.

16 times I felt the burning sting of Propofol injected into me. 16 times my body heaved upwards on the bed as a rubber mask was shoved into my airways. 16 times my brain was shocked.

Electroconvulsive Therapy. ECT. The root of my adulthood trauma.

I was 5 years old when I told my mom I wanted to kill myself, I was 7 years old when I was given mood stabilizers for adults, and I was 14 years old when I was diagnosed with bipolar 2. I was 21 when I overdosed for the umpteenth time, I was 22 when I almost had organ failure from it, and I was still 22 when I had ECT.

These surgeries were the last attempt at saving me. My doctor's exact words. I accepted because I wanted help; I finally wanted to be saved and there was something that could change my life.

Electroconvulsive Therapy is where a certified doctor places nodes on your head, turns the dial on the little blue box to the correct voltage, then shocks your brain and gives you an induced seizure for your brain chemicals to change.

My head was full of negative thoughts and lightning strikes.

I was young. I didn't question things. I wasn't in the state to ask if it was humane or why only a handful of the doctors in the US perform this surgery. Why grown adults sat in the ECT waiting room each day, crying for the procedure and for themselves.

There was minimal communication between doctors. There was no communication between the advising doctor and my mother. Words were sparsely passed to those who needed them, but whispers of my too long seizures were talked amongst nurses.

16 brain surgeries were a lot. 16 brain surgeries were too many. 16 brain surgeries caused me to lose parts of myself.

I had amnesia. I was given it on a silver platter. I couldn't remember my past and I couldn't think of certain words. My parents believed ECT was a miracle while I was screaming for someone to hear me inside my own head.

There is no way to prove whether these surgeries worked or not. My mother says yes. But my mother is not me. She is not 30 years old and still cries for her 22-year-old self when an IV is put in her arm. She doesn't have flashbacks of the smell of the rubber mouth guard or the trauma of laying on a cot, naked from the waist down, while 10 people hold you as you thrash and crack a rib on the railing of the bed.

I am better than I was. The brain is still a mystery and there is no amount of prodding that I would go through again if I had the chance. I used to weep for what I went through.

I no longer cry about it, though. Now, I write about it.

I Want Someone to Love Me

Sexuality is a scary word for a lot of people. Society has seemingly let everyone know that the normal sexual procedure is to be heterosexual (straight) since the beginning of everything. I'm being a little dramatic on the timing, but as I'm a dramatic person in general, I'm saying it's true. Being heterosexual is what has been around for a while and what has been accepted for too long of a time.

Homosexuality (gay) became the next greatest acceptance. Gay pride and free to love who you love. There are still people who don't accept homosexuality because they're still stuck in the ways of everyone being heterosexual. Yeah, that's *still* going on.

As much as it pains certain people, time goes by, and sexuality starts to broaden. There are different umbrellas of preferences and what people do and do not like. Bisexuality is very prominent in today's culture, which is where you like both men and women. I assure you that at least one person walking down the city street next to you is either gay or bisexual. It's probably more than one person, but I'm ever the drama queen.

There is one sexuality that is just now starting to get talked about but has yet to pick up a wide acceptance.

Asexuality.

Asexuality is the lack of sexual attraction to others. It can also be low or absent interest in (or desire for) sexual activity.

When I was younger, I always had crushes on boys. I'd like to shoutout Sean from 5th grade and Jon from 6th and 7th grade. I had a crush on Will in 10th grade and his girlfriend for a month always gave me a knowing look in the hallway.

I was definitely a straight white female. I didn't know anything different, and I knew I wasn't gay. As I approached adulthood, I still had crushes on guys but...that was it. Thinking of getting intimate with someone made me outwardly cringe. As in, if I thought of kissing that cute guy at my friend's party, I would dramatically get the shivers. Most of my friends know about the guy in my early college career that I wanted to date. He didn't even like me, he just wanted the attention. (HI KYLE! DON'T EVER SEND ME ANOTHER "Heyyyyy" IN THIS LIFETIME!) But I refused physical contact with him, even though I liked him at the time.

What was WRONG with me?! Why couldn't I have sex with him like he wanted? It would have been a great time, rolling around on his oddly out of date waterbed, watching The Perks of Being a Wallflower.

Was I broken?

That was a big word that lasted a long time in my life: Broken.

As I entered my early twenties, I still didn't know what was wrong with me. There *was* something wrong, though, I was sure of it. There had to be. I haven't even had my first kiss and by then, my friends were getting married and having kids. I blamed it on my weight, I blamed it on how my face looked and I blamed it on the multiple men in my adult life that told me I was ugly.

But did I want to get married? Did I want to date? Did I even want to make out with someone?

I looked deeper in myself and talked it out in therapy I told my therapist I didn't know who I was, and I just felt...different. And not even a cool different.

I then concluded by myself that I was bisexual. Women were beautiful. They had luscious hair and nicely shaped faces. But I wasn't really *attracted* to them. I then tried to place my gender into my sexuality at the time. I wasn't informed that there was a difference and then I kept thinking "maybe I feel like a man?" This was a soul-searching thing that took some time to figure out since there was no Map of Megan, and I had to teach myself later that gender and sexuality are different things.

I was just as confused as ever because I didn't like ANYTHING. I didn't want anything!

I came across the phrase "asexual" on Google. I don't know what I searched but it popped up, along with the definition. I was petrified to give myself another label. I already thought I was a ton of different ones and I yelled to the world that I was bisexual (my fault.) But asexual really seemed to fit me. I told my mom about it, and she was confused, of course, because being asexual isn't "normal" (hello heterosexuality, my former friend.) She didn't know what it was, so we talked about it, and I was absolutely enthralled when my mom said "Yeah, I see that in you."

A few years went by and here's the comments I received when telling some people who were close to me, that I was asexual:

"So... you're like a tree? You just...exist?"

"Oh, you'll change your mind one day!"

"You're just insecure with yourself. Once you lose weight, you'll like yourself more."

"You haven't explored enough to know your sexuality."

I stopped telling people. I kept getting hurt. I was in my late 20's; was I supposed to start my promiscuous phase soon? Each time someone inadvertently told me I wasn't who I was meant to me, my heart sank into a puddle of pain. Then it brought up the fact that, if I really was asexual, I would never give my parents grandkids or a son in law or a white picket fence fantasy. My mom deserved that white picket fence.

Having sex is the only way this world turns.

Right?

I just didn't understand one thing: why is me being asexual such a burden on other people's lives?

I still get butterflies when I like a guy, which is called Heteroromantic. I like men and have happy feelings when I like someone, but it's rare. Except, I don't want to have anything past that, which is where the asexual part comes in.

I just want everyone to know, especially to those who are questioning why they don't have great grandkids by now: I can have a fulfilling life, too.

I have married friends who are asexual. Two of them, in fact! Yes, you can get married and love someone while being asexual. Everyone is different and so are sexualities.

I went to a Pride bar crawl in 2021, in my little hometown that has 13 bars within walking distance. I wore an Ace (short for asexual) colored bandana around my wrist. I bought it in June that year at Target, which is when they sell their pride gear and make a profit off of it. I never wore it before because I had no idea why I even bought it. I was the only one who was wearing those colors, but I wasn't judged for the first time in my life.

A girl I know came up to me later in the night, after a few drinks were consumed and said, "I didn't know you were asexual" and I had the whole "I don't tell anyone because everyone gets upset at me" speech and this girl looked me in the eyes and goes "You need to be who *you* are. I accept you."

That girl and I don't talk anymore because I don't even know if we were ever real friends (she's really funny, though, so I'm jealous of her actual friends) but I will never forget her saying that, even if I was a little tipsy.

I used to cry every time I talked about my sexuality. It's not something I want, and I still find it to be a bit of a burden. I would love some company occasionally, you know? But dating is all about hook-ups these days and we know how well *that* would go. I have to learn to live my life. I'm already badass; I can only go up from here.

Bar Hopping

B Bar was the most popular bar by my house when I was 22 years old. My friend and I called it a college bar but there aren't really any colleges around, just really young people.

B Bar was my first taste at an unrequited high school reunion.

Girls I used to be friends with would dress in miniskirts and heels and make their entrance down the steep stairs with their posse in tow, not once looking in my direction. My early college days best friend was once there and she pretended I wasn't sitting at the table she passed, wearing my cute leopard print blouse, and my dyed green hair. Most of the girls and guys I went to school with that occupied B Bar made it awkward to enjoy myself there. At 22, I wasn't ever planning on going back to my high school days.

I tried going to other hang out bars in the area but never found one I liked. I went one that is now a popular with couples, but it was weirdly empty back then when I went and uncomfortably so. I tried out a so called "nightclub" type of bar one time and it had a terrible DJ. It was also full of old men that just got out of work and couldn't stop drooling over my underage friends who got in with a fake ID. People my age usually had their go-to bar by then and I just couldn't find "the one."

In 2019, I had a friend group that took me to another local bar that I didn't know was even in the area: 2 B's Bar. There are seemingly a lot of bars with the multiple letter "B" around town. I walked in the place for the first time and the openness of it immediately caught my attention. I wasn't pushed up against a stranger's shoulder that smelled like Axe body spray, and I wasn't yelling when I told a story to the person next to me. They had pool tables and dart machines and cornhole games. It was a place where I didn't have to dress in kitten heels, and I could have a conversation with friends over drinks at an open table.

I started to feel comfortable. I was frequenting 2 B's with different friends and over the years I have ordered endless Apple Pie Shots and Liquid Marijuana's (which is rum and a liquor that turns your drink bright green.) I grew closer to the owner, who is the type of woman to watch out for you if you need it and she supports me in ways I never expected. When I went back to college, she was happy for me. When I got offered a summer internship, she was there cheering me on. There's no better feeling than having sparked up a friendship from an unlikely place.

I'm not a continuous drinker by any means, but I think I go to 2 B's Bar for a sense of comfort from the people there. The owner, the bartenders she's hired and the nonjudgmental patrons. I dress cute sometimes to go there, but not because I feel obligated to, like the other bars, but because I was feeling it that day. If I see people from high school at this bar, they say hello to me. It's a different type of atmosphere and it's one I'm honored to contribute to.

I finally found my go-to.

Hired

I don't think the word "desperate" suits me as a person, but in 2021, I was desperate. I had been at my current retail job for 3 years and I was fed up with a lot of things. I no longer wanted to cry each Christmas season because of all the stress I was put under, and I was tired of customers acting like I wasn't a human being, no matter how nice and helpful I was to them. I had been in retail my whole life and I always said, "I'm good at retail, I just don't like it."

I applied for any and every desk job I could at my 2.5-year mark. I started applying in 2020 but no one would return my application emails. I was a fantastic worker and even though this would be a new path for me, I was eager to learn. Not one call back. I started getting some phone interviews finally the next year and I learned why no one wanted to hire me: I had no experience. These days, you need to come out of the womb with 5 years job experience. It's over the top and no one is willing to train anymore; you have to go in knowing what you're doing. And I, of course, didn't. One interview was so awkward because the woman kept asking me "are you sure you don't have any front desk experience?" and I had to keep reiterating to her that no, I don't but I'm excited to learn. I never heard from her again. I had at least 6 interviews in from 2020 to 2021. The last interview I had was the one that stuck.

My mom saw a front desk job opening online for a new senior living community. I applied, not expecting to hear back. The description fit me well, but I really only applied to make my depressed state a little lighter. Somehow, I got an interview. It was April 2021. The woman who interviewed me was desperate at the time as someone just quit and I was desperate, too, and I landed the job. She was willing to teach me what I needed to learn and that was miles above other jobs already. I started in May 2021.

I could make this essay about how much I love my coworkers and how much the residents mean to me, but that's already all said by now. This is a dedication to the woman who took a chance on me. As the community grew, so did I. Each time I came into work, I never know what's happening until I was there. My coworkers saw me get stressed and anxious about my job sometimes, but they know me and they know I can get through a hard day. But my boss, the lady who hired me, is who I can rely on. Not in the way where I can't do things myself, but in the way that she knows I can do them. She sits in her office across from my desk and I sometimes think about the time she took a chance on me. In return for my desperation, I found a job that changed my life.

I should really thank her. But this short essay will have to do for now.

Riding Along

Being in the back of an ambulance was exciting when I was a kid. We would get to see inside one of them when we had a field trip to our local fire station down the street. Us young, impressionable kids, would be amazed at how cool those trucks where.

Being in the back of an ambulance was not exciting as an adult. Laying strapped to a shifting cot while paramedics hooked me up with wires and shouted to each other "still can't find a heartbeat," was boring. No excitement happened like I always thought it would. Adult Meg was severely disappointed.

The best part of this frantic ambulance ride was that I got to witness all the stoplights turn from green to red as we sped past all the cars. Just for me.

I never heard about if they ever found my heartbeat.

Take it Back

There's a word that annoys me and this word is always pinned to my back like I enjoy carrying the weight of it: *strong.*

Looking up the definition online, "Someone who is strong is confident and determined. They are not easily influenced or worried by other people. Strong objects or materials are not easily broken and can support a lot of weight."

What Google doesn't describe is the way that people throw that word at you when you tell them about your life or your past. "Wow, Megan, you're so strong for going through all that." I get so agitated, and I always went to yell the truth back: "I'm not strong, I was born this way and I went through hard times because I was forced to." I didn't choose to have a lifelong bipolar diagnosis. I didn't want to suddenly find that I have a form of ADHD as an adult. Taking medication after medication because other people couldn't handle me or being driven to therapy as preteen so my parents could get a break from my constant anger. It was a difficult time, but I didn't have a say in any of these decisions.

On Thursday, April 6th, 2017, I wrote a blog post on my lifestyle blog. It was titled _Ladies All Across the World._ I named the post after a girl-power singing group called Little Mix, who sang catchy songs of empowerment. To this date, it is my highest viewed blog post on that very small website. By that point in my life, I was fed up with hearing I was 'strong' about my past, but then I started questioning that word used around my present identity. 500 people read my blog post that I wrote where I said: "I'm not a strong woman. I post about fundamental rights on Instagram, but I don't go to women's marches because of my anxiety in huge crowds. I was told I couldn't attend shop class in high school because I was a girl, but I never stood up for myself. I'm a fraud." I was no longer thinking about my life choices that were chosen for me. I was now a young adult who was living in the time of female encouragement, and I didn't feel like I should be anointed with the cliché label of "strong woman."

For that blog post, that I didn't make money on and was only writing for fun, I interviewed people who identified as women and I asked the question: "What does being a strong woman mean to you?"

"Not being afraid to be weak or ugly- and owning the things I find embarrassing" said digital media artist, Molly Soda, who was popular on Tumblr.

"Being a strong woman means being vulnerable, honest, and open," which is what a Hollywood industry model told me after I reached out for a quote.

But there were also quotes that my friends, who were not celebrities, gave me. They said things about celebrating other women and being able to know yourself and your standards. Some of the quotes I agreed with and some of them I didn't. But did I have a place and a right to disagree? My favorite interview was with my friend, Natalia:

"Being a strong woman means that I can endure social justice with great fortitude. It means I don't give up. It means that I am passionate and I'm able to express my individuality. Being a strong woman means sticking up for our rights, our bodies, and the equality we deserve."

As 2017 has passed and it is now 6 years later, I don't dwell on the word "strong" like I used to. The only reason being is that because no one says it to me anymore. I don't think I miss it in the context of my past, but no one says it like they did in my younger years. There then came a point in my life that I realized I don't need to dwell on the label of being a strong woman. If someone sees me that way, I commend them. But as a grown adult, I don't get offended or angered when someone calls me something I believe I'm not.

I Only Date Celebrities

I wore a shirt that says "I only date celebrities" to a One Direction concert in 2015. It was the only clothing item I had that was clean during that depressive stage in my life. It was white and old and probably had pit stains. After getting a little tipsy at the concert on some kind of fruity beer, I sobered up when my friends and I found out what hotel Harry Styles, a beloved band member, was staying at. I'm not quite sure how we found out, but apparently, we had a good source.

When the concert was done, it took about an hour to get out of leaving the arena traffic, but it was fine because it made sure Harry would get back to the hotel. We found the hotel, parked our car in a sketchy lot, and got out.

My two friends and I saw some other young girls there and they were dressed in low cut tops, carefully smeared on lipstick, and hair that was most likely extensions. So, in short terms, they fit in while I wore a stained shirt that screamed, "**I'M A**

CELEBRITY STALKER." My friends and I were not very good at sweet talking security, and I was the most unattractive one there, so it was going to be a very difficult mission, getting us all inside. All of us girls, even the ones we didn't know, were standing around the parking lot, discussing plans on how to get in. It was odd to me that we were the only ones there. Normally, it would be swarmed with people. Maybe it was the time of night? Maybe, just maybe, it was the wrong hotel?

We saw some patrons come out of the front door of the hotel, which was still guarded by security, talking amongst themselves about a "stupid boy band member in the hotel." So, it seemed to be the right hotel, now how to get in to see Harry. I was the only real adult in that group, although I looked 18 years old. But let me tell you, I didn't even think about how maybe Harry wanted to sleep and be left alone; I've loved him too much not to be selfish at that point in time. Somehow, I was the one that got pushed into asking the grumpy security guard at the door if I can use the bathroom inside. I was nice about it, he was not. He told me no, and that there were no bathrooms anywhere nearby. I went back to the group, obviously defeated.

While I was gone, the girls we just met had made some "friends" with the creepiest guys you would ever see. They led us across the street and told us that there was a bathroom in the bar there because we really did need to use them. When we went back outside, the creepy guys kept asking the obviously underage girls if they wanted to go back to their place. The girls kept going, "Oh, maybe. Should we? I don't know. Should we?" When the guys had enough of the girls' indecisiveness, they left, and we still hadn't gotten into Harry's hotel. I was getting impatient because I was tired, and in all honesty, this hotel might be nice inside, but it was situated in a strange place in Chicago that was under construction. Also, Chicago at night is never a good idea.

Someone had the bright idea to sneak around the guard and go and see if there was a back door. We made sure that one lone security guard didn't see us, and much to our surprise, there *was* a door, but without an outdoor handle. Suddenly, a hotel worker who came outside for a smoke break, came straight out of that same door. He propped the door open with a stopper and turned around and looked at us without words. There was a cute girl my size in our group with huge assets and she automatically started flirting with the guy. "Can we get in? Why not? We won't do anything baaaaddd." I couldn't hear their whole conversation because I was standing a little farther back. I was trying to hide myself and my shirt, and if we needed to run away fast, I'd have the easiest access. But the girl kept flirting and kept tugging down her shirt so low that if any more skin was shown, it would be blurred on television.

Eventually, the hotel worker waved us inside. I was hesitant for a second. Did he mean all of us? Even me? I was the last one to go through the door, and suddenly, I was in the same hotel that Harry Styles was in. I was in his atmosphere. I was an adult woman, sneaking in through a back door to share air with my favorite person I have never met. Then it all ended quickly when the girls in front of me were running back and pushing me out, saying, "Go! Go! Go!" When I was once again outside, I spoke up: "Did someone kick us out?" And the girls replied, "No, we just got spooked." I just stood there. I literally did not move. The worker said bye and went back inside, and the door was closed. I was still unmoving. I couldn't BELIEVE we got that far, and those girls got "spooked." My friends and I got back into the car to drive home without even saying goodbye.

I didn't meet or see Harry, but we pretty much shared the same breath. Maybe. I mean, I was down in the kitchen and God knows where in the hotel he was, but we both were breathing at the same time, I was sure of it. So, to Harry Styles, as the odd one out in that group, I tried my best. It was scary, it was kind of fun, and I didn't end up in jail.

My Letter to Bookstagram

I joined a new community August 23rd, 2020. I posted a photo of a small stack of books on my new Instagram page that I aptly named Megan's Booked Up. I used to have an Instagram page once where I tried to be an "influencer." I would get free product and promote it for more free products. But it was a harmful community of people who only liked you if you were pretty and if these content creators didn't get enough people following them, they would post videos of them crying and blaming Instagram. I didn't like the pressure I was under, and it was all for free things I probably would never use. When I deleted that influencer account and switched over to a book account, my first post received 31 comments from strangers saying, "Welcome to Bookstagram!" I didn't know this side of social media was going to be so welcoming.

Bookstagram was the book side of Instagram, and I was immediately thrown in a whole new world. There were authors, and advanced readers copies, and book reviews galore. I posted pictures and wrote captions about what I read and what I wanted to read. I started making friends online and I started turning my real-life friends into book lovers. I don't use filters anymore to make my page look aesthetically pleasing like I used to when I first started, and I really only take pictures of the books, not my face. I didn't want to go back to the pressure to be perfect like my influencer Instagram. I'm not on social media to please people anymore; I'm there to have a good time.

In the 2.5 years since I've joined Bookstagram, I've started my own book podcast, I met online book friends in person, made a book club and joined a few, I've talked with and made friends with authors, and I wrote this book.

How undeniably exciting.

If I could, I would name each person I have met because of books, but that would be a long list. I am floored when people say they read a book because I recommended it or they message me, praising my writing. I wanted to say thank you to everyone who has cheered me on and supported me these past two years. This short love letter is for all of you.

Now go read some good books.

Just Another Manic Monday

I like to compare my age to what was going on in my life at the time. Years pass me by, but my age is what matters.

I was 14 years old when I was diagnosed with bipolar 2. It seemed so big to me at the time but now it feels so insignificant that the English language won't even let me capitalize the word. I was never happy like those with bipolar 1. I didn't want to pack my bag and hitchhike to California, and I didn't feel like opening a credit card and buying a condo all in one day. That was mania. The difference is that my bipolar came with a big 2 scratched on every evaluation form. Every caregiver told me that I won't have mania and every doctor never mentioned manic episodes.

And I didn't have them. At least not until more than 10 years later.

There was a day when I was 26 years old and the snow on the ground glistened with the sun shining on it. It was a cold January day, but it was beautiful.

My friend Ashley and I were on a portrait picture taking kick that year, so we went out and took photos in the snow. We took pretty pictures of each other, all bundled up in our cute winter clothes and pretended we weren't shaking from the single digit temperatures. We took at least 120 pictures each and when I saw mine after we were all done, I thought I looked great. I saved the good pictures, deleted the bad, edited my face a little skinner, put a filter over it, and stared at myself on my phone. Ashley was a good photographer, but that fakeness of the filter really made me look beautiful for once in my life.

I went home after the excessive posing for pictures and by then, it was nighttime. I got ready to sleep, laid on my bed, and posted my pictures of the day on social media. I was going to wake up the next morning and see if there were any comments, but instead, I immediately got a notification on my phone that someone did comment on my pictures. I then got another notification. They just started pouring in, the comments and the likes.

"Megan, you look beautiful!" was written many times. I have never been called that, so it was a shock to my system. I knew my pictures were heavily edited, but it was still me in the picture, so I took the credit and ran with it. I posted more pictures of the day on my accounts. The more compliments I received, the more I was getting jittery, but I thought it was a good thing. I put my phone face down on my bedside table, then went back to laying on my bed. My phone sounds were off, but it only took a minute and a half to check to see if anyone else complimented me. It started to become a game: how long can I go without checking my phone?

During one of my very short "not checking my phone" times, I realized that my mind was racing so fast that I couldn't think straight. It was like my stream of thoughts were coming out in one line and there were no breaks or paragraphs, no commas or periods at the end of any sentence.

Then, my arms started to tremble.

The shaking in my body worked its way up to my chest. It felt as though the inside of my entire body was vibrating and I was half expecting my bones to make an audible rattling noise. My heart thumped to a beat I didn't recognize, and it got really hot in my room all of a sudden. The first thought I could think of after noticing this phenomenon was: "I have to check my phone."

It didn't occur to me to ask someone for help because all I wanted was to see who else called me pretty. I started a new Instagram account for those pictures because I wanted to take more. More, more, more. I was gulping for air at the same time as I was smiling with my teeth.

I stayed up until 6 a.m. and then I eventually went to sleep somehow. When I woke up, I finally had enough reasoning to say, "WHAT THE HELL HAPPENED TO ME LAST NIGHT?" At the time, I didn't seem to worry about my body's response. I just worried that I was looking good on Facebook. I Googled my strange symptoms, as one does, and it came up that I had a hypomanic episode.

"Hypomania are periods of over-active and excited behavior that can have a significant impact on your day-to-day life. Hypomania is a milder version of mania that lasts for a short period."

I was told that this wouldn't be a problem for me. I was also a grown adult who had never once had that happen to me in the 12 years since my diagnosis. I could always question "why me" in everyday life, but with this experience, I wanted to only question "why now?" I hadn't even heard of hypomania until I Googled it, which was concerning a little bit. I went to my psychiatrist whom I've been with for years and told him quickly of what happened.

"Oh yeah, that can happen. If it lasts more than 2 days, you need to be hospitalized."

Why would I need to be hospitalized? Because my brain turned on a mode I'm not used to? But that was that and it was never talked about again because I didn't have any more episodes for that whole year.

It was January as a 27-year-old, almost exactly a year later, and a family member sat me down and told me they wanted to talk to their husband about his addiction problem. This family member was afraid her husband would leave her, and she would be without money (the husband was money hungry) and without a place to live. This person had been telling me for years how miserable she was with her husband, even if she didn't see it. When she told me about her future confrontation and the years of me being her unpaid therapist came to a head, I spiraled.

I ended up in my small room that night, pacing back and forth on my carpeted floor for 4 hours straight. The tremble started in my chest this time and it went to the tips of my toes. My brain was giving me fight or flight signals, but I was stuck with this mental issue, and I didn't know how to cope or even how to combat it. I frantically went on Google to see if I could get my family member into a domestic violence shelter, but she only suffered mentally by her husband; I didn't know if she would be taken in.

I paced, I Googled, and I shook.

This is something I can never truly put into words, but when your brain has a hypomanic episode and you *know* you're having one, it's a feeling you wish you never had to experience. I don't even think about if I had true mania because that is something I can't dwell on.

4 days. I had that episode for 4 days. To some, that's not many. To me, it never ended. I was manic at home and at work. I asked my coworker/friend, who I knew also had bipolar, how to deal with it. How I could get better. She told me I couldn't do anything to help myself, I just had to wait it out. That was terrifying to me, doing this all alone. I didn't tell my family and I didn't tell my doctor because I didn't want to be hospitalized. I knew nothing about this type of mania still, and it felt like everyone who walked by me didn't see me. No one noticed I wasn't myself. I couldn't ask for help

because what could they do for me? I didn't shed any tears because my brain was too focused speeding up a notch every 5 minutes.

It's almost been 3 years since my last hypomanic episode. I don't know if I'll ever have one again, but it scares me that I don't know what triggers it. I can be overly happy or extremely overwhelmed. There's no pinpoint and when I think about it too hard, it can feel like I'm walking on eggshells.

I never want to live in fear of something I can't handle.

What is Love?

It was 8th grade when I sent a boy I had a crush on a personalized valentine for the first time and last time.

His name was Kyle. I had sent him a school valentine where you paid a dollar and on February 14th, they get delivered to the designated person with a note you wrote on it. I had liked Kyle for 2 years and I got a weird nerve on February 13th, so I finally went for it. I bought a valentine for him, I wrote a note that said, "I don't know why I'm sending you this, but here you go," then signed my name. Valentine's Day came and he had it given to him at the end of class. Which I had completely forgotten was a class I was in *with* him.

I can still picture the place he sat that day, on the blue metal chair, his friend's crowding around him trying to read his Valentine note, and me staring at him so hard out of pure shock that I was going to witness his reaction.

Then, he laughed.

I can still hear it ringing in my ears because of how loud it was. He passed the note I wrote specifically for him to everyone within reaching distance. I sat across the room and watched with utter horror as boy after boy laughed at me and my handwritten Valentine. I was hurt and embarrassed. I felt so vulnerable that I wanted to both throw up and cry. Kyle never said a word to me for the rest of the year.

I haven't spoken to him since I was 13 years old, but I tried looking him up online 17 years later. He has no Facebook account, and I can't find if he has an Instagram under a different name. I found his LinkedIn and saw he works in IT. I then noticed his profile picture, as a man in his 30's now; a grown up. My heart lurched at his oddly angled picture but not because he's my type (which he is very far from now), but because I didn't know how much I still mourned for Middle School Meg's heart.

Kyle was the first boy who let me know I was ugly, and it only got worse from there.

*

Each time I had a crush on a boy in high school and the boy found out, they treated me like a pariah. I was ignored and never spoken to again because they were embarrassed an "ugly girl" liked them. It wasn't like I was picking the most popular and hottest guy in school to like; they usually were nerds with shaggy hair. Apparently, the egos of nerdy 14-to-17-year old boys are bigger than you expect. But each time a friend of a friend of a friend spilled the rumor of me liking a boy, I was reminded that I was overweight and not particularly nice to look at. My funny personality didn't matter at that age.

After my cystic acne went away senior year of high school, I thought everything would change. Except nothing did because I was still 175 pounds and had a chunky and round face. I went onto college without ever having been kissed or having anyone have a twinkle in their eye when they looked my way.

I had yet another boy named Kyle (there are just so many of them in this world) capture my interest when I was 18. I was infatuated with him because he was the first ever guy to show me sort of interest, even if at the time I didn't know he was an awful person. I latched on to it and waited by my computer every night for him to message me and make my heart flutter. Kyle never asked me to lose weight, but he always played mind games with me and never outright told me he liked me. I decided to shed some pounds to see if my crush would finally be reciprocated. I lost 30 pounds for him and not once did he notice.

I finally cut College Kyle out of my life and grew up with cliché body dysmorphia. I hated my appearance because everyone else did, too. I was the "fat ugly friend" with each friend I went out with. My friends would always get hit on while I was standing right there. Being ignored by men was something I was used to, but it still hurt. An (ex) friend had a boyfriend in 2019 that said he wouldn't stand near me nor speak to me because of how I looked. I was too overweight and I had an unappealing face, he said.

I was in my mid-twenties when I joined my first 2 dating apps. I took great pictures for it but there was no way to hide a double chin and round cheeks. I had 2 matches in my 2 months of being on those apps; one guy that was strange and the other one was a spam robot. I deleted the dating apps because of how it made my adult self-esteem go straight downhill. No one wanted me, even if it was online.

You'll hear men constantly say, "I like a natural woman with a great personality" and then you'll hear me respond with "you're a goddamn liar."

I'm tired of people telling me that I'm too extroverted to be liked by a man or that I have a wonderful personality only. Older people tell me how pretty I am, but the younger ones won't say anything back when I bring up my insecurity. Why can't I be beautiful? Why am I not worth it because I take so many medications that make me gain weight? Why do I deserve to be the highest recipient of loneliness?

I'm 29 years old and I've given up. I will never get married, so I tell everyone I don't want to get married. I will never like a man so much that I get the honor to hold his hand. I will never be able to show off my cooking skills to someone who appreciates me for me. I will never know what romantic love feels like. By the time I'm 35, I'll hopefully be settled with all this but for now, I deeply hurt.

Tell Them That It's My Birthday

The best part of a birthday is the wish you make when you blow out the candles.

For all my 29 birthdays, I've felt different for each one. When I was young, July 25th was always full of birthday parties my mom put together and friends came to celebrate me. I loved being the center of attention, the star of my own show for one day a year.

Middle school was when I started really thinking about my birthday candles. In 6th grade, I began to wish for what I truly wanted. I would be seated at our kitchen table, my mom taking pictures of me and my cake with the family digital camera, and me waiting for the annoying birthday singing to be over. I leaned over and without thinking of it beforehand, I wished for what my heart desired:

"I wish to be happy."

All through middle school and high school, I wished for the same thing. To be happy and to live a life I loved. Each year that passed, it wasn't coming true, but I still blew out those birthday candles with my fake smile meant for show and my identical wish.

When I was in my late teens, I realized that I needed to change my birthday wish. I started dreading my birthdays and I was angry I was still alive, much less getting older. I started wishing for things that didn't matter because I had given up on ever being happy.

I was in my mid-twenties when I changed my view on birthdays and life in general. I started celebrating that I was still here and not in a grave. I threw my own birthday parties with friends and always included a pinata if it was held outdoors. I was surrounded by people that loved me and didn't know the history of my birthday feelings.

My 29th birthday came, and I didn't know what to wish for. I was sitting at the same kitchen table, with my mom taking pictures of me on her phone, smiling a genuine smile when my family sang happy birthday. When it was time to blow out my candles on my homemade cookie cake, I hesitated for a bit to think of what I truly wanted that year. I finally made a wish and blew out the candles.

I can't tell you what I wished for on that birthday, but I can tell you what I didn't wish for. I didn't wish for happiness. I thought it would be silly to waste a birthday wish on something I finally have.

I Feel

I feel inadequate.

I don't think I fit here, in this class, along with these people who live by words and who learn by words. I was forced into this experience but everyone else here chose it.

I feel less than.

     Less than their personalities that group together.

     Less than their minds that figure everything out.

I don't think a piece of writing is deep. I put them in 2 personal categories:

good

and

bad

The good: It was easily written to flow as I read.

The bad: There is a deeper meaning, hidden for those who always seem to know.

English can be critiqued, just not by me.

I can't see the underlie.

I can't read the message.

I feel inadequate.

What Happened to Zack?

Grief is not something I ever thought I'd have to deal with. My mom, Amy, was 31 years old when she had me and my maternal grandparents were both gone by the time I was in kindergarten. My grandma Muriel died from breast cancer when my mother was 11, so she never had a mom to lean on or learn from. My own mom still mourns, all these years later.

My dad, Kevin, was 23 when I was born, which was an 8.5-year difference between my parents. My paternal side was thriving in the fact that I had two living grandparents and a really cool step-grandma (who I called "grandma" because the "step" part didn't matter to my heart.) My dad's side was who I was closest with, even at a young age. No one seemed to die, and everyone was happy.

I started attending funerals in college. I had been to some before college, but in my mind's eye, early college is when it started to become bigger than myself. I went to the wake of my old neighbor and another one for my detached first cousin. My best friend's mom and brother died, and I attended all that I could to support her. I was lucky, it seemed, that death never surrounded me too much and I didn't lose anyone too close to me by that point in my life.

But then there was Zack.

OBITUARY

"Zachary, age 24, of _____ passed away on Sunday, October 8, 2017. Zack was born in IL on May 18, 1993. He was a lifelong resident of the area and a 2011 graduate of _____ High School. Zack was employed as a Karate Instructor at _____. He was a National and International Karate Competitor and held memberships in the AAU and USANKF. Zack was a huge supporter and volunteer for the Green Tara Program. A program which helps teach

self-defense to at risk women in prevention of Human Trafficking."

"What happened to Zack?" was a text I woke up to in October of 2017. Lisa, the woman who texted me, was close with Zack and I in high school. Zack, the kid who wore a Hannah Montana backpack to school and wasn't even ashamed. Zack, the quiet yet smiley guy who sat with me 2 times a week outside my community college class to keep me company before I went in. What happened to Zack?

I saw him a week before October 8th, 2017. He was out walking his dog and I was taking a walk to get my exercise in but didn't really want to be seen because I looked awful. Yet, there comes my neighbor and childhood friend, Zack, strolling along the same sidewalk. "Oh God, hi Zack. I definitely didn't shower so don't look at me. I'll see you soon, though!" He smiled, chuckled, and told me he'd see me soon, too. That was the last time I ever talked to Zack.

Zack died by suicide on a Sunday. The next Saturday I was attending his funeral. Most of my friends who were also friends with Zack had moved away at that point, either for college or to start a new life. On October 14th, 2017. I dressed up in a black dress, brought a change of clothes to go to work right after, and drove by myself to the local funeral home.

Death was new to me. Grief was even newer. I wished I had a partner or someone at my side as I pulled my car into the parking lot, already having my eyes briming with tears. You can drive yourself crazy with asking "why", so I didn't at that moment in time. I also didn't fully accept that he was gone, especially in this way. I opened the heavy wooden door and walked past the mingling people in the lobby. I didn't know a single person. I didn't even know what his dad looked like until he introduced himself to me. "Did you know Zack?" he asked. "Yes," I replied. "He was my friend for many years. I loved him."

After saying my sympathies to Zack's father, I was holding it together well at that point as I walked into the big room, the room that Zack occupied. It was an open casket. I've seen an open casket before, but I have never been affected by one as I was with Zack's. I didn't walk up to it right away because I wasn't ready. I sat down on a chair at the side of the room and gazed at the "in memoriam" picture slide show on the wall. It was playing a scene of more recent pictures of him, and his head was full of medium length blonde dreadlocks. I don't know how much I paid attention to the rest of the pictures, as I was preparing to go up to the casket when it was cleared of people kneeling and praying. No one paid any attention to me. I was just the girl alone in the corner, mourning her childhood.

As a few tears started to slide down my cheeks, I picked myself up, and walked to see Zack. The exact last time I would ever see Zack. I reached the casket, stared down at my friend, and gave the saddest smile I could never muster again during my lifetime. "They cut your long hair, my friend. You look just like you did in school." I don't know how long I stood and stared at the boy I undeniably loved, but I don't think time mattered at that moment. That was the precise minute my first ever encounter with grief started.

I pulled myself away from the casket, away from Zack. My heart felt like he ripped it out and put it in his pocket to bury it with him. I went back to sit on my chair, I pulled out tissues from my purse, and I wept. I cried for his family, I cried for his friends, and I cried for his pain. I got up to leave and walked over to say goodbye to his dad. As I told him how much I treasured Zack, his dad pulled me into a hug that wrapped us up together in our grief. I cried harder on his shoulder as I whispered repeatedly: "I'm so sorry."

I walked out of the funeral home, I unsteadily went back to my car, drove to work, and cried again in the parking lot before I went in for my shift. I called my mom and told her how much he had hurt me. My mother, as she still mourns *her* mother, told me to think of all the good things about Zack. I sat in my car, listing things I will miss about him, all with my mom's help. I went inside, changed into my work clothes in a dirty bathroom stall, then started my long shift, thinking about Zack the whole time.

I got home from work that night when it was dark, and the stars were shining through the clouds. I pulled myself wearily out of my car, walked into the middle of my front yard, and fell on my back. I laid there, I looked at the beautiful twinkling stars and asked aloud: "Why? Why would you do this to me, Zack? I don't deserve to lose you." Grief took ahold of me, heart and soul, and I cried until the last star that night snuck behind the rising sun.

The Push

I finally got standing general admission tickets. My favorite band, The 1975, was playing at a venue that was huge and was popular in the Chicago area. And I, Megan, got pit seats for the first time in my life. They weren't that expensive, and I always wondered if that was my karma for being a nice person in life, getting these tickets.

I waited in line for hours, like a typical fan, since seat numbers aren't given for standing room. I didn't sleep in a tent overnight or get there 3 days before to line up, though. I find that craze a little bit strange. I wore my cute faded black Target jeans with pastel flowers embroidered on the sides and a white top that said, "Poison Me Daddy" that I got from their online merch store. It was a lyric from one of the band's songs.

I got my wristband after hours of being antsy but then we had to wait even longer to get into the actual the venue. Baby steps. I had undiagnosed diabetes at the time so I couldn't figure out why my feet were tingling so much while standing so long. I had the problem before, but they were getting bad that day.

The doors eventually opened, the tickets were scanned, and people were already pushing each other to get through the double door entrance. Then everyone ran. There was the stage, and it was a timed sprint to the barricade. Whoever won the competition, they got the gold medal of front row. The closer to the band you were, the more bragging rights you thought you got.

I got 3rd row. I count that as a bronze achievement.

By that point, my feet were in so much pain that I couldn't stand still, shifting my feet every 3 seconds. My feet felt like they needed to be cut out of my shoes or just dramatically cut off in general. I wasn't in the best mood anymore and the bands ended up coming on late. The first two opening acts finally performed, and they we're not great. I just wanted to see my band then go home.

After waiting so many hours to see a person sing songs, The 1975 eventually came on the stage. Then it all happened at once: everyone in the audience went out of their minds. The rush of fans who were pushing towards the stage was so intense that I couldn't breathe. Their hands were shoved up in the air as if the lead singer would actually notice them and they acted like I was a random rag doll, made to be thrown. I've been to smaller standing shows, but never one this completely feral.

This particular concert had more males in the crowd than I've ever had at any other shows I've been to. They were the main ones pushing and when I had the frantic chance to look around, they were the ones laughing because they thought "the push" was hysterical.

I couldn't move. I couldn't breathe. I started crying. No one would let me through to the back of the mob. For the first time in my life at an event, I started having a panic attack, right in the 3rd row of The 1975 concert.

Dye Job

I don't like change, but I will willingly participate in it if it's on my own terms.

In middle school, I had natural blonde hair. A beautiful spun gold color when I was a child that ended up dirty blonde by the time I was 12 years old. My mom let me highlight my hair in the sun with lemon juice and then I got accidental brown streaks in my hair in 7th grade. Some people called me "skunk," but it didn't hurt me because I agreed with the nickname.

I wasn't allowed to dye my whole head per my mother so in high school, I started with the chintzy blue and purple clip in hair extensions. I had long hair past my shoulders that turned a darker color as I aged. Then during my time in community college, I had my friend dye my first ever blue streak in my hair. A permanent reminder of how great it felt to have color in my life.

I experimented with box dye, as young ladies who don't have a lot of money do. It was always darker colors but never on the spectrum of black. I would let the brown colors fade, then do another one. I felt like it was something in my life I could creatively control.

The pictures of me during my first time going bleach blonde show a girl who is excited but didn't know what the hell she was getting herself into. A boy semi broke up with me (were we even dating?) and I was 18 years old. I officially didn't need my mother's permission to change my own life. I went to my friend's house, she bought bleach from the local hair store and had no credentials on how to apply it, but she did anyway. The moment it touched my head, I was a whole new woman from there on out.

From that bleachy moment, I started dyeing my hair funky colors. Purple with blue underneath, light green streaks in my blonde hair, then I dyed my whole head an aqua color. I got so many compliments on that color, and I was called "Blue Haired Megan" for a time. Whenever my mother got mad at me, she'd call me a Smurf. When she wanted to compliment me, she called me a mermaid. There were so many fun colors I experimented with, and it made me feel pretty and strong.

It was around my first time at university when I box dyed my hair black. I didn't like myself and I was in my dark and moody phase. I did it in my school apartment bathroom right over my bleach blonde hair. It was then I realized that my hair color matched my moods. I felt a sense of power in that. I had cut my hair with art scissors, gave myself straight bangs, and dyed.

When it was time for me to change my very cheap black color, I did something that would make every hairstylist scream and yell: I bleached my own hair right on top of the black box dye. I had no idea what I was doing, but I knew better. I felt that it was time for a change again and I wanted to try incorporating my favorite hair colors back into my life.

I have never gone back to black. I also now have a job that says fun hair colors are not professional, even if the residents I work with would love it. I have been bleach blonde for years at this point. I used to call myself a peroxide groupie, but blonde makes me happy. It reminds me of my spun gold childhood. My hair is now naturally a dark brown color and I think it's the muddiest color known to the world. I don't like it and will always dye over it until my deathbed. But as a wise woman once said:

"Blondes have more fun."

Concrete Heart

There was a long moment in my life when I never spoke about what was on the inside of me. I grappled enough on what was on the outside too much to pay attention to the rest. I would use the word "no" to everyone in power, I would wear combat boots into holy sanctuaries, and I would lay on my bed and stare at the walls for hours in hopes to get at least one tear out. I was a fighter; I was a rebel; I was hurting.

There would be times where I would go to forced doctor's appointments and I said nothing. There were other appointments where I told the doctor about how I liked cute celebrity boys, that I went to a midnight movie premiere with friends, and how I liked to read a little bit. It didn't help me enough. The doctors were there to get paid. I was there so I couldn't end my misery.

I was given therapy homework and I was put in centers where we filled out worksheets full of writings that told us how we should get better. I spent my time in multiple hospitals, reading books my parents smuggled in to pass each waking and painful moment. With every day and night, the sun and moon ran together. There were still no tears, still no feelings.

*

5 years have passed from then and that means 5 years in recovery. The time in between those years were full of brain surgeries, flowers given as unspoken thoughts, and a simple crack in my double dipped concrete heart. Right down the front valve. There was no blood yet, there was still no life, there was just air. The beginnings of breath in my lungs starting to bloom.

*

The pandemic came and showed me that extroverts had a hard time surviving. I drank alone in my room while I danced alone in my room. Night upon night, I mixed vodka and rum. Then day upon day, I was lonely. I tried getting help and while I called one doctor after the next, I got turned down by all of them. They were too full of patients because 2020 was a difficult year. They couldn't help me, and they didn't want me. I still hadn't cried.

*

I bought a book in the spring of 2020.

The Gift of Forgiveness: Inspiring Stories from Those Who Have Overcome the Unforgivable by Katherine Schwarzenegger Pratt.

A nonfiction book, something I usually only read for school, never for fun. I saw it advertised on my least favorite talk show, The View, and as my mom turned it on every day at 10:00 a.m., I left the TV room every day at 10:00 a.m. That day in March 2020, I was unfortunately sitting and watching The View. I had just gotten over a crippling sickness that led to me finding out I had adult diabetes. I was physically sick, and I didn't want to admit it, but mentally I wasn't doing too great again. As I sat there, staring blankly at the women yelling in condescending tones at one another on national TV, a daughter of a well-known family was introduced as an author: Katherine Schwarzenegger Pratt. Katherine spoke about her new book and about how she interviewed people. She asked the hard question no one wanted to talk about: what did forgiveness mean to you?

Something in my heart told me to buy it.

*

My mental sickness along with my physical sickness made me lose interest in things including life itself.

But I bought a book.

That meant I would have to read it. Which was a something that could lead to a hobby, or I would want to read more books, or it would possibly mean I liked things again. It was immaturely overwhelming. Was I helping myself? Was I getting better once again? I used to read when I was younger, but as an adult, books seemed to be something I could not enjoy anymore.

I finally received the book in the mail after ordering it as soon as could. I had bought it with my laughably small Target discount I got from working there. I held the brand-new book in my hands and felt the smooth hardcover under the dust jacket. The green and white colors with the little picture of a wrapped package on the front went well with the title.

I went upstairs to my room, I laid on my bedsheets that hadn't been changed in a while and covered myself with my One Direction blanket. I opened the book to the introduction and for the first time in 10 years, I read.

*

"No one can process a hurt like yours, what it'll mean to you, or how it'll affect your world."
-The Gift of Forgiveness: Inspiring Stories from Those Who Have Overcome the Unforgivable by Katherine Schwarzenegger Pratt

*

It was 11 p.m. when I finished the book. It was 11:01 p.m. when tears fell. It was 11:07 p.m. when I sobbed.

I hadn't cried in 6 years. I always told myself that my medications were the things that kept me from showing emotion. But that night in March 2020, my heart had finally shattered the concrete around it, all by itself. The little hardened pieces were swept away by my lungs gasping for air. Tears ran down my face and onto my blue Anakin Skywalker cotton shirt. I cried for the people in that book, I cried about the heavy subject matter it covered, and most importantly, I cried for myself.

*

After finishing The Gift of Forgiveness and when my tears had dried as salty trails upon my face, I grabbed my phone. I opened my Notes App and composed a hasty a note. A note to those who had hurt me in the past and to those who I didn't know how to forgive.

"I know we haven't spoken to each other in years, and you may never see this message as we are not friends on Facebook, but I just read a book. It was about forgiveness and even though I always thought I was bad at forgiving; I think this book changed me. I know my past isn't who I am, and I know we've all changed as people, one way or the other. But I wanted to write you this message and let you know I forgive you."

I sent this message to 4 people.

I waited for instant responses that never came. I thought about how a single book was the cause of this. Of this abnormal event. Of this relief. My heart needed some new stitching in certain places, but it felt like it was a fresh start. A healthy start. I suddenly hoped my mom would forgive me for all the distress I had put her through, and I hoped my brother would forgive me for putting it on him that he had the chance to save me.

I shut off my phone for the night as I kept checking for messages that would eventually never come, snuggled in my dirty sheets, and spoke aloud from the new air I found in my lungs, to myself, for myself:

"I forgive you."

You Got a Friend in Me

There was Robyn. I met her when I was 5 years old at a new church when I moved to Illinois.

There was Candice. I met her in 5th grade, and we solidified our best friendship after she accidently sneezed on my festive Halloween shirt.

There was Megan H. I met her in middle school and when we changed schools, we became email pen pals.

There was Nicole. I met her in graphic design class during my first round of community college.

There was Ashley. I met her at the mall when I was in college and although we went to high school together, I didn't know her.

There was Lindsey. I met her in 2013 at an airport while we were looking for celebrities to take pictures with.

There was Lauren S. I met her when we shared a school apartment together at university and I only lasted a semester there.

There was Noe. I met him at our job in 2014 and we became instant friends after talking about our same favorite bands.

There was Maddie. I met her in 2020 through a Twilight Pen Pal sign up form on Instagram.

There was Paisley and Ally. I met them at a Harry Styles concert in 2021 when Paisley spilled his beer on my friend and Ally looked into my eyes and sang Watermelon Sugar.

There was Lauren G. I met her when I joined her online book club in 2021.

—

There's a rumor that goes around when you're young: when you grow up it's hard to make friends and it's even harder to keep them.

Don't believe everything you hear.

—

There is Robyn. I called her from the airport in New York when I was on vacation because I thought I was having a diabetic emergency. She helped me through it and calmed me down.

There is Candice. I interviewed her for my podcast and all we did was laugh and reminisce and even though that recording accidently got deleted, it made me smile all week.

There is Megan H. She lives out west now but our annual tradition of getting together for breakfast and exchanging gifts for Christmas when she comes home each December is my holiday miracle.

There is Nicole. I'm about to travel to Seattle with her on vacation soon; our first time as adventurous travel buddies.

There is Ashley. We see each other as much as we can and she is a part of my family, even if we're not related.

There is Lindsey. I take a solo 6-hour road trip once a year to visit her, usually for her birthday, and we end each of our videos we send each other with "I love you and miss you."

There is Lauren S. I attended her wedding and we mail each other Christmas gifts each year. She handmade me a reading journal for 2021 and it was the best gift I've ever received.

There is Noe. We see each other at least once a month (most of the time more than that) and after almost 10 years of friendship, he still puts up with my random spontaneity.

There is Maddie. She flew from California to Illinois in fall of 2022 to visit me and I showed her around the Midwest. She is one of my best and supportive friends.

There is Paisley and Ally. We sent each other Christmas cards in 2022. I took the card down from where I had it taped to my door and placed it in my memory box.

There is Lauren G. She came to Chicago in 2022 and I'll be flying to her in 2023. Her and her family make me believe in fate as it was a sign of love that I met them.

—

There was a song we would sing in Girl Scouts that had lyrics I never appreciated until now: "A circle is round; it has no end. That's how long I want to be your friend."

Loving Greg

His name was Greg.

I think he has a last name that starts with a G or an S, but it's been so long that the more I think about it, the more of a probability that it was actually any of the other 24 letters of the alphabet. I tried typing Greg G. and Greg S. in my Facebook search bar a couple times in my life. Greg Green? Greg Smith? I just really wanted to find him.

I was 15 years old when Greg and I met. I was from a growing town in Illinois, and he was from somewhere else in the US. I think if I knew the state he lived in, my Facebook searches would be extraordinarily easier. We both traveled to South Carolina one summer with our respective churches to help repair houses. Our small church called it a Mission Trip, but I never thought to question the actual name of the program.

In 2008, we took a road trip to the south with my best church friends, loaded down with bags full of candy that the church members put together for all of us, and an inner turmoil of teenage self-hate. That was normal for me: pretending that everything was fine to outsiders, even though every part of me was in mental anguish.

When we reached South Carolina after our 2-day drive, we were split up into groups with other kids who were purposefully not from our own church, for our day activities. I got put in a group of teenage strangers; 2 boys, another girl, and the only non-youth, a leader in his 40's, who we called Coach. If I'm not mistaken, and I usually am, one boy was named Taylor and the other girl was also named Taylor.

But then there was Greg. A skinny, blonde haired, blue eyed, 16-year-old who had a smile that would make you blush. And if you got to know his sense of humor, you would blush even harder.

Greg wasn't vulgar in any sense, at least not the Greg I knew. He would make you laugh one second and then as soon as you stopped, he would randomly climb the nearest tree, just to see you smile again. By my first day of knowing him, I knew he was way past charming. Greg was endearing.

He started to pay attention to me quickly. Me, a 15-year-old with a head of badly dyed short brown hair and acne lining her face like a pirate's map. But Greg saw the treasure in me, and I don't know how or why.

I let Greg into my life for that week and told him secrets about myself. I would love to know what all I spoke of, but I did tell him about my love of the Jonas Brothers, my favorite boy band, and how I really wanted to be an actress. He listened to me like I mattered.

I didn't get many pictures taken of me while I was on that trip. I was insecure about how I looked, and I absolutely hated the face I was given by God. Every time a camera flashed, I snuck out of the frame. I, of course, don't remember if I ever told anyone my reasoning for no pictures, but I think Greg might have picked up on it.

The other girl who was in our group (Maybe Taylor) had long, wavy hair and was a natural beauty. The Boy Taylor was also very good looking for a 14-year-old, with his chocolate brown hair always sticking out of his backwards baseball cap. I think I felt a little out of place, not because they weren't kind, because all I received was pure kindness from them, but because I didn't look like them. I always told I wasn't pretty and at that age, I felt it.

Greg got mad at me for the first and last time that week. The program that we were a part of put on a skit each night correlating to a passage in the Bible. The people in the program who ran the theater portion put out a notice that they were looking for "actors" to help put on a skit for the night. Greg thought this was my chance, my big acting break. A starring role as Mary, Mother of Jesus, in room full of sweaty and bored high school kids who just wanted to go back to their rooms to gossip and sleep. He begged me and pushed this opportunity on me like I was someone important to him. He didn't understand that I couldn't do it, not with how I thought I looked; I was more fitted for a character with Biblical leprosy. Greg didn't know me. After bickering back and forth, I finally said no and walked away from him.

That night, the same one that should have brought me fame and future roles, I sat a few rows behind Greg. He was with his church group, and I was with mine. Separate lives and separate emotions. As soon as the nightly skit started, Greg turned. His bleach blonde head somehow knew exactly where my seat was, and his blue eyes blazed into mine. As he sat staring me, his face was a scrunched-up sea of waving emotions. He was angry at me that I didn't participate in the skit. He was upset with me because he wanted to see me act. He was hurt because I told him no.

Why did Greg even care?

He and I put the emotions of the night behind us and the next day, we both acted like nothing happened. The days of working and sweating in the South Carolina sun came and went by too quickly.

We laughed with each other and we made a sweet connection with the tenants of the house we were working on. At the end of each Mission Trip week, you can write nice notes to your new friends and stick it in their big, designated envelope with their name scribbled right on the front. You don't have to sign your name; you just have to be kind. You also don't get to open your special envelope and read your messages you got until after the last day is over. I filled out many for friends I would never see again, Taylor, Taylor, Coach, and of course, Greg. I don't know what I put on my message to him, but it was probably a joke of some sort. Nothing too heavy.

I gave Greg a hug goodbye for the last time. He wanted me to add him on Facebook, but I wasn't allowed to have one. I wrote down his full name so I could add him when I finally made one in the future and gave him mine.

I lost his last name and he never looked for me.

I used to call Greg the first boy I ever loved. But that's not really true. It wasn't a teenage love that got away. There was nothing romantic there. I think Greg was the first boy who listened to me. The first boy who really showed me I was more than I thought I was, and that I was worth caring for.

It's been 15 years and I still think about him. I wonder if he is married with kids or if still uses that sly smirk to bring joy out of people. I only want to think good things of Greg's future because I know I would be emotionally devastated if it wasn't. I have made Facebook posts and Tik Tok videos to help me find Greg these past years, but nothing helped. In 2013 I found a disposable camera I apparently brought along during that 2008 trip. Most of the pictures were too old to develop, but two pictures of Greg showed up. One was where he thought he was a model and gave me a serious pose, and the other was with him and I; me giving a cute tilt of my lips and him giving a full-blown grin. I don't ever remember taking that photo, but I wish I had more of them.

*

On the card ride home from that year's Mission Trip, I tore open my envelope with all my kind messages. I sifted through them and saw one from Greg: "I hope you're famous in the future and you get to go swimming in a pool with the Jonas Brothers!" He signed his name at the bottom of it and I smiled. After reading almost all of them, I picked up the last one. With a curious look on my face, I saw that it had only two words on it:

"You're beautiful."

The "b" was looped, and the "t" was crossed and there was no signature written. I stared at those words for a while. Blue scratchy ink on white printer paper.

The same handwriting as Greg's.

Halfway There

I cleaned my room the other day and dived beneath my bedframe, throwing my hands out like a fishing lure trying to grab onto the junk I've shoved back there way too long ago. I came to the surface with 6 notebooks; 2 of them with badly written poems about how sick I felt, scribbled on the first 3 pages that I wrote when I has a strange autoimmune sickness in 2020. The other 4 were cute reading logbooks where I wrote my progress on books I finished, along with other book topics. I wrote to page 5 in one of them about how my current book club I founded was thriving. Another was a 2-page list full of books I started and refused to finish because I found them so boring. I stacked those unfinished notebooks into a pile on my off-white carpet, that severely needed some cleanup work done, against the wall. I've vacuumed my room before, of course, but never fully. I rarely get out the vacuum hose and sweep up my crumbs against the wall crevices. I take another glance at the notebooks that I would most likely just push under the bed again with my unopened Blu-ray copies of my 2nd favorite TV show, Misfits. I don't even own a Blu-ray player.

I have a 2011 Ford Fusion. A dependable one, although if you ask me what makes it dependable, I'll probably just say "it gets me places." No one can ever get the color right. Is it green or is it blue? It's not a full color. The car manufacturers painted it with the thought in mind that a young girl in 2017 who lived her life in halves, would buy this car. The best part of my car, named Annabeth after my Percy Jackson series obsession in late high school, is that it has a skip button for the aux on the steering wheel. I plug my phone in each day into the charging cord that is severely bent in half, and I listen to my favorite band as I prep for my day. Then I use the skip button that is conveniently so close, before the end of the song happens. I do that with each song I listen to. I don't even let Harry Styles finish his last line in "Watermelon Sugar" before I skip to the next song.

Each holiday, my mother tries to make sure my tissue boxes match the season. I find tissue boxes so bulky and unappealing in a décor setting, no matter how festive. But I use them, nonetheless, and make sure the top tissue sticks up like it's reaching to the ceiling, for aesthetic purposes. When I get to the bottom of a tissue box, there is a lump of them curled over each other, begging me to put them out of their ugly misery since they can no longer provide the fullness like a beginning box can. I pluck out the bottom ones, open a brand-new box, then push the old ones on top of the brand-new tissue and fluff them up. I can't ever finish something fully.

I call myself a "creative soul." I take up hobbies like I won't live to see another day. I made choker necklaces from colored rubber bands for about 2 months straight. Then I started churning out yarn friendship bracelets that took up my time for about a week. I found a pair of jeans that I cut a hole into and started sewing around, creating some sort of pattern. I stopped sewing in the middle of a weeping, yellow flower petal that was placed above the left knee.

I attended a total of 3 years of college in my late teens and early 20's, in hopes of becoming an artist. I started at community college, wanting to go into graphic design because I knew that would make me money in the art field. No matter what anyone tells you, art school is all about comparison and I am a sensitive human, as it turns out. I created things that schools didn't appreciate. I wasn't a cookie cutter artist and I loved it at the time. But the teachers didn't, and I had a hard time finishing school projects because of it. But I kept on my way to getting my general education degree finished.

In my free time during my early college years, I would work on the weekend as a sample girl at a grocery store. Many times, when we had to cook the food first, I would burn it in the toaster oven we were given. I ended up passing out cut up burned pizza slices because half of my shift was already over. I started an Instagram called DIYMANIA where I gathered a following of people who enjoyed my crafts I made. I deleted it after I never kept up with it. I started to learn how to play guitar and I could strum the first few chords of an old Bon Jovi song, then I grew too bored to learn the rest.

I decided to apply for a traditional art school before I graduated with my associate degree. I got in, which was a complete shock. I didn't even finish my general education classes yet. I lasted one semester at that university art school then I dropped out. No degree in my hand to show my hard work, just advice from a teacher telling me that I was bad at every aspect of art, and I should change my future. A college dropout only sounded good when it was placed on my "always started, never finished" repertoire.

After school came and went, I dabbled with the idea of going to beauty school, but I found out that I'm not good at doing my own makeup. I only apply eyeshadow to the bottom half of my lid, although the tutorials on YouTube tell me that the pigmented powder is supposed to go even higher. I used to love dyeing my own hair and I would combine hair colors into one mixing bowl: half purple and half silver. When it was time to rinse out the dye under my showerhead, I never washed it all the way because I would tell myself "If there's still some in your hair, it'll make the color seep in stronger."

The best part of a cup of home-brewed coffee is the first forth of it. I make a light roast coffee and switch between my favorite coffee mugs, one with a picture of a pair of lips I received during my 3-year obsession with lip prints, and one that says, "I dated Pete Davidson and all I got was this lousy mug." The type of coffee switches from caramel to vanilla to whatever is currently cheapest at the store. I drink my hot coffee during my morning social media scroll each day and when it's halfway gone, I get up from my recliner and pour it to the top once again. I have been to that terrible place where the sludge at the end of the cup condenses together, and it has those bottom dwelling grinds swimming around like angry piranhas. I refuse to go back to that bitter place. So, after the pot of coffee has run out, I dump my almost empty mug into the sink and prepare for the second half of the day.

Acknowledgements

I always hate when this end chapter just names people in a paragraph. It's just so...long. So instead, I'm going to separate my Thank You section, because it's my book I can do what I want.

—

My mom, Amy. Thank you for advocating for me when I couldn't love myself. There are traces of you in this book without ever mentioning you. You are my #1 supporter and my best friend. Love you, mama.

My Bookstagram friends. I wrote a whole dang essay for you all, but you guys keep me going. It goes past just books now, it's in "I LOVE YOU SO MUCH" territory. Your support for a book about a small-town girl AKA me is phenomenal. Thank you for your love.

To all my residents. I can't name each one of

you because some of the red tape there but there are too many to name anyway. Thank you all for being excited when I tell you things about me and for always hyping me up. I have a small immediate family, but I now have a big family that includes you all. I love you, my dear community residents.

To myself. I always like to put this dedication because I'm so proud of how far I've come. If I were to tell my 16-year-old self that I love my life and I love everyone who is in it, I wouldn't believe you. But it's true. I'm almost 30 years old and it's been a heck of a ride. Thank you, Megan.

To everyone who is reading this. Nonfiction these days isn't popular, especially essay books from someone who is not a celebrity. I appreciate each and every one of you who read this book. I hope an essay, a story, or even just one quote resonated with you. You are loved, not just by me, but by the world. Thank you, friends.

About the Author

Megan is big fan of coffee, Harry Styles, and flowers. She hopes one day that Harry Styles will bring her flowers to the coffee shop they meet up at.

GET IN TOUCH WITH MEGAN HUBREX:

Bookstagram: @Megansbookedup

Email: Mhubrex@gmail.com

Made in the USA
Las Vegas, NV
07 April 2023

70342312R00069